7288

D1710219

AMY CARTER
Growing Up in the White House

by Alma Gilleo
illustrated by Helen Endres

THE CHILD'S WORLD

ELGIN, ILLINOIS 60120

Library of Congress Cataloging in Publication Data

Gilleo, Alma.
    Amy Carter, growing up in the White House.

    SUMMARY: Describes President Carter's daughter's
life in the White House.
    1. Carter, Amy—Juvenile literature. 2. Presi-
dents—United States—Children—Biography—Juvenile
literature. 3. Carter, Jimmy, 1924-   —Juvenile
literature. [1. Carter, Amy. 2. Presidents—
Children] I. Endres, Helen. II. Title.
E874.C26G54   973.926´0924 [B]   78-7812
ISBN 0-89565-028-2

Distributed by Childrens Press, 1224 West Van Buren Street, Chicago,
Illinois 60607.

© 1978 The Child's World, Inc.

Amy at her father's desk in the Oval Office. Amy's
brother took this photo.

Have you ever wondered what it would be like to
live in the White House?

Amy Carter could tell you.

Amy gets a ride into the Governor's mansion. This
picture was taken in 1971.

Amy lived with her mother and father in Plains,
Georgia. Her father grew peanuts on a big farm close
to Plains. Plains is a very small town. Amy had lived
there all her life, except when her father was governor
of Georgia.

Amy liked living in Plains. She liked to be with her friends.

But Amy's father wanted to be President of the United States.

Amy with her mother and father. This picture was taken a short time before her father became President.

In November of 1976, Mr. Carter got his wish. The people elected him President.

Amy cried when she heard the news.

"Didn't you want Daddy to win?" her mother asked.

"Yes," said Amy, "but I don't want to go to Washington. I want to stay in Plains."

Soon after New Year's Day in 1977, Amy and her family said good-by to their friends in Plains. And they moved into the White House in Washington.

Amy liked her pink bedroom and her playroom. She found just the right places for all her toys.

People in Washington wanted to meet Amy's father. They gave many parties for him. Amy got some new clothes. She wore them to some of the parties.

Do you remember your first day at a new school? The night before going to her new school, Amy went to bed early. She wanted to get up early the next morning.

Amy's mother went to school with her that first day. The Stevens Elementary School is just six blocks from the White House. Amy had to ride to school in a car, so the secret service men could protect her and her mother.

Newspaper reporters and people with cameras were waiting for Amy at the school. They took her picture and wanted to ask her questions.

Amy smiled and waved. Then she hurried into school.

On the door of the classroom was a big poster. Some of the children had made it.

Amy loves ghost stories. So on the first day at school, she told a funny ghost story. The boys and girls liked that!

Amy liked her new school. She liked her teacher, Mrs. Meeder. Soon Amy made new friends.

Claudia Sanchez became Amy's good friend. They always sat together on the bus when the class went on field trips.

Claudia and her family had moved to Washington from Chile. That is a country in South America.

Amy found that there were fun days at Stevens School. One day, 20 girls from the Soviet Embassy School visited them. The girls did some Russian folk dances. One girl asked Amy to be her partner. The two girls danced the Virginia Reel, an American folk dance. That was a fun day!

Often, some of the children at Amy's school stay after school. They stay because they want to. Amy stayed after school three days a week to learn how to speak Spanish.

Amy dances with Luba Borisova, from the Soviet Union's Embassy School.

Another day each week, Amy stayed to learn how to take good pictures.

The children at Stevens School planned a special program for their parents. Amy took some pictures to show what students do in school. She helped write the story of the Stevens School.

President Carter came to the program. He saw Amy and some other girls do a dance. At the end of the program, President Carter gave awards to 30 children. Each child had done well in physical fitness classes. Amy got an award.

Do you have a pet? Amy has more than one pet.

Amy's teacher gave her a puppy named Grits. Grits was born the same night Mr. Carter was elected President.

Amy has a pet cat named Misty Malarky Ying Yang. She calls the cat Misty for short.

The Carter family has a dog called J.B. That is short for Jet Black. They have a parakeet named Blueberry.

Amy wanted a tree house, so her father drew plans for one. It was built on tall wooden legs, or stilts. It is not really a tree house, because it is not nailed to a tree. But Amy and her friends must climb the tree to get into the tree house. Even President Carter climbed up for a visit one day.

Because Amy's father is the President, she is asked to do some interesting things.

Amy was invited to the National Zoo in Washington. A country called Sri Lanka wanted to give a baby Asian elephant to the zoo for the children of America. Amy thanked the people for their gift to the zoo.

Many special visitors come to the White House. Amy has met kings and many other important people. Sometimes people bring her gifts. But Amy can't keep all of the gifts. They are put in a special museum, so everyone can see them.

Mr. Brezhnev, of Russia, sent Amy a set of Russian dolls.

And one gift Amy especially liked was a white helmet used in the movie, *Star Wars*. Mark Hamill gave her the helmet when he visited the White House.

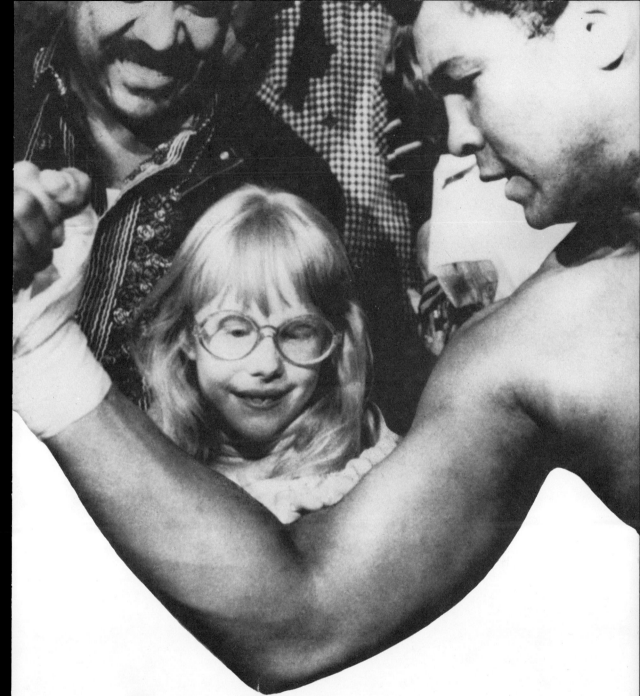

Amy and her classmates went to see Muhammad
Ali. He was at his training camp. He was training for
a fight with Alfredo Evangelista. Do you think Amy
liked that trip?

During her first summer in the White House, the Dixie Liners came to a lawn party. They did some mountain dances. Amy liked that. She likes to dance.

Living in the White House can be fun, Amy learned. There is a bowling alley, where she sometimes bowls with her famous father.

There is a movie theater there, too. Amy invited some school friends to come and see the movie, *Freaky Friday.*

There are lots of books in the White House. Amy likes to read ghost stories and stories about animals. She also likes to read books about science.

After supper, Amy and her mother often read in the White House library.

Amy learned something special about the White House. It has a secret stairway. When a certain wall panel is pushed, the wall moves back, and there is the stairway.

Some people say there is a ghost in the White House. Amy asked her friend Claudia to stay all night with her. They slept in the big bed Mr. Lincoln used to sleep in.

The next morning, the girls giggled and said they had heard the ghost. Do you think they did?

Amy likes to play in the big yard around the White
House. In winter, she loves to have snowball fights
with her mother and big brothers.

Amy is glad her father is President of the United States.

But sometimes, there are things Amy doesn't like about being the President's daughter.

She can't just walk to school with her friends. Wherever she goes, secret service men have to go with her.

Newspaper reporters ask her lots of questions. People take her picture. Often, they stare at her.

Do you think Amy sometimes wishes she could just ride her bike down the street? Or walk to the store alone?

The President's child cannot do these things in Washington.

GARFIELD SCHOOL LIBRARY
LONG BRANCH, NEW JERSEY

29

Amy likes to dance and play and watch movies with her friends. She likes to do all the things other children do.

But, most important, Amy is always herself. Some day, she will go back home to Plains, Georgia. But for now, Amy Carter has fun in the White House.

Amy with her nephew.

All photographs in this book are used with the kind permission of United Press International.